What's in that Egg?

A Book About Life Cycles

BY

BECKY BAINES

NATIONAL GEOGRAPHIC

Washington, D.C.

Hey!
What's in that egg?

Is it
a turtle?

Turtles are reptiles.
Reptile eggs can be hard
but are sometimes soft
and leathery. Some reptiles
bury their eggs.

A frog?

Frogs are amphibians. Amphibian eggs are like jelly. Some are laid in strings, others in bunches.

They need to stay wet, and are laid in ponds or streams or even in leaves that hold water.

A fish?

Fish lay lots of eggs at a time. Most let their eggs scatter in the water. Some freshwater fish make nests underwater in the sand.

A butterfly?

A butterfly is an insect.
Most insects are tiny.
Insect eggs are teeny tiny
and hidden!

Or a swan?

A swan is a bird.
Birds lay hard-shelled eggs
in nests to keep
them safe.

One thing's for sure, though an egg seems so small ... there's a whole world inside. It's a home after all!

Home Sweet Home

Some babies live in eggs
for only a few days.
Some live there for months.

Albumen

Shell

Yolk

Inside the egg,
a baby floats ...

Albumen makes up most of the egg.
It allows the growing baby to float
and not get bumped around!

1

2

... growing in size
while eating the yolk ...

The yolk is the food that the baby eats
to make it big and strong.

3

4

... getting bigger and stronger 'til suddenly ...

Tap! Tap! Tap!

5

6

... ready or not that egg's going to HATCH!

8

7

Most baby animals "tap" open hard-shelled eggs.

Eggs can be

Apple Snail Eggs

pink!

Cassowary Bird Egg

Or green!

Robin Bird Egg

Or blue!

Some eggs can even be see-through!

Glass Frog Egg

Long and skinny, pointed or round?

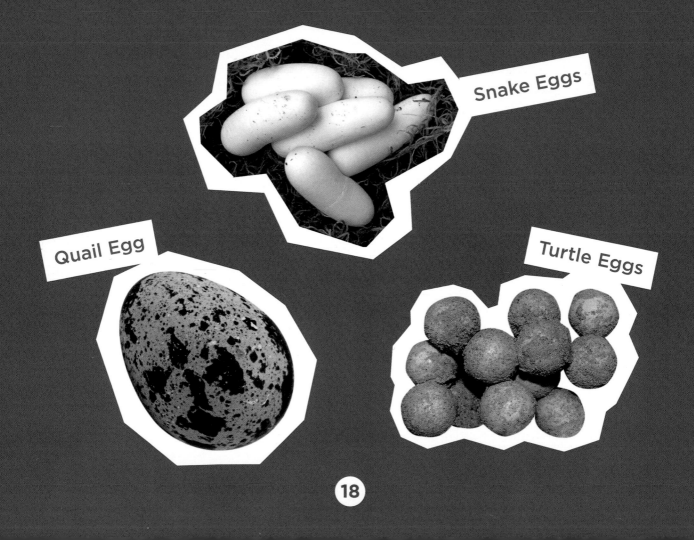

Snake Eggs

Quail Egg

Turtle Eggs

All different shapes of eggs can be found.

Guillemot birds lay their eggs on narrow rock ledges. If the eggs were round, they might roll off the ledge. Their shape keeps them safe.

Guillemot Egg

19

Ostrich eggs
are the largest
of all eggs.
They can get
as big as
$7\frac{1}{2}$ inches tall.

Bigger than a cantaloupe, or too small to see,

Hummingbirds
lay the smallest
bird eggs!

They are only about
one-half-inch long.

Emperor
Penguin Egg

**there may
be just one,**

The eggs an animal
lays at one time
is called a clutch.

Clownfish Eggs

or 2 thousand, or 3!

Is it hard?

Is it soft and leathery?

A baby is born!
Do you know what kind?
The egg might tell
what was growing inside.

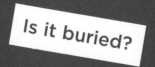
Is it buried?

Is it underwater?

24

Happy Birthday, Alligator!

Alligators are reptiles.

26

They have soft and leathery eggs, which they bury under leaves or sand.

Zigzag through these ideas for more thoughts about life cycles.

Cut open a hard-boiled egg. The white is the albumen, the yellow is the yolk.

Where was your home when you were born?

If you were a bird, what would you build your nest with to keep your egg safe?

How do animals know when it's time to hatch?

If you had an egg, where would you put it to keep it safe?

When you were a baby, what did you eat to get big and strong?

Shine a flashlight into an egg – you can see inside!

Make a nest for yourself!

If elephants laid eggs, how big would they be?

Roll an egg across the floor and see which way it turns.

Why don't all eggs look the same?

Why don't all animals lay eggs?

National Geographic's net proceeds support vital exploration, conservation, research, and education programs.

Published by the National Geographic Society
1145 17th Street, N.W.
Washington, D.C. 20036
Visit us online at www.nationalgeographic.com/books

Design: fuszion

Printed in the United States of America

Library of Congress Cataloging-in-Publication Data

Baines, Rebecca.
   What's in that egg? : a book about life cycles / by Becky Baines.
      p. cm.
   ISBN 978-1-4263-0408-8 (hardcover : alk. paper)—
ISBN 978-1-4263-0409-5 (library binding : alk. paper)
   1. Embryology—Juvenile literature. 2. Eggs—Juvenile literature. I. Title.
   QL956.5.B35 2009
   591.4'68--dc22

                            2008047895

Photo Credits
Corbis: 7, 8, 12, 13, 16, 18, 19, 20, 21, 27
DK Images: 5, 11
Getty: 14, 15, 25
iStock: 9, 18
Jupiter: 6, 22, 30
Minden Pictures: 17
Nature Picture Library: 26
Sea Pics: 23

To Johnny & Liz
- a couple of
good eggs.
—B.B.

See ya later Alligator!